This book is dedicated to all the mentors I've had in my life, both physical and from the spiritual realm, far too many to name as the list would be book length. This book is also dedicated to my inner strut, the deeper part of me that I have finally begun to pay close attention to.

CONTENTS

Introduction 1

Part I: Warrior Woman Ancestry
Warrior Woman Ancestry:
    The Ancestral OG Strut 9
The Evidence and the Truth:
    Strut Origins and Fabrications 11

Part II: Personal Strut
Early Years 21
My Middle Name and Hints of My Inner Strut 27
Obstacles for My Strut: Beliefs................................31
My Personal Ancestral OG Strut:
    My Maternal Grandmother................................35
Single Mom vs. Peeping Tom:
    A Warrior Protects Her Family 41
The Wrath of a Petite Dynamo:
    Small Frame, Big Strut..45
The Necessity of Creativity...................................49
Until I Get Tired: Warrior Wisdom.......................51

My Journey as a Woman Warrior

LEARNING TO RESPECT MY STRUT

KAREN TAYLOR

Synergy Publishing Group
Belmont, North Carolina

Learning to Respect My Strut: My Journey as a Woman Warrior
Karen Taylor

Published by Synergy Publishing Group, Belmont, NC

Cover by Arielle Torkelson
Interior layout by Melisa Graham

Softcover, December 2023, ISBN 978-1-960892-10-2
E-book, December 2023, ISBN 978-1-960892-11-9

Pool Halls and Obligations:
   A Warrior Doesn't Honor Irresponsibility............55
My Parents and Their Influence on My Strut........59
I Have a Big Chip on My Shoulder 65

Part III: The Dream Strut
Before the Dream Came True:
   The Strut Emerges 73
My Dream and the Rise of the Strut 81
Female Cop, Patriarchal Crap:
   Wielding the Strut...85
Problems from the Women
   Unaware of Their Strut..93
A Comrade Down: The Angry Strut.......................99
Being a Cop and Having a Life:
   Strut Contradictions 105
Afterword: From Personal to Universal 115

Preview for Book II 117
About the Author 121

INTRODUCTION

I have spent my whole life trying to be a man. It's not my fault.

I'm done.

This book shares my sixty-two-year journey full of "learning" that in order to be valuable and successful, I had to exhibit masculine characteristics. Let me explain.

Despite writing this book in 2023, and despite the abundance of women's movements and achievements in all aspects of society, we still live in a male-dominated, patriarchal society. Since I was born in 1961, my childhood was fraught with even heavier constraints of those barriers than we have today.

I was born in a small town in Western North Carolina in the foothills of Appalachia. When I was three, my family moved to a somewhat larger town in South Carolina. In the time period and area that I grew up, I experienced many rules that governed women on behavior, dress, and speech. The rules seemed to influence so many aspects of my life, from what sports we were allowed to play to what and how much we could eat. I was taught that being a women meant

 … wearing my hair a certain way
 … being slim
 … being polite
 … being quiet
 … being feminine
 … being small
 … being a sexual target
 … fitting into the feminine box

As I grew up, I quickly came to realize that I didn't want to be put in the box that I was taught was my place. I also observed how my male counterparts were *not* being asked to fit into these same types of boxes. They seemed to have more freedom. So I decided early that if I were more masculine, then I was protected. Guys wouldn't mess with me if I acted tough and cussed, for instance. My early years were spent on a seesaw, up and down, between an attempt to conform to the expectations of women, hitting bottom, then pushing back up and resisting these expectations by being a "tomboy" and doing everything I could to be the son I felt my dad had truly wanted (more on that later).

As I grew older, my rebellion grew with me, and I exerted more and more energy in trying to be a girl who did whatever a boy could. It took a long time for me to understand myself and what I was really trying to do. You see, though I didn't recognize it at the time, what drove me was an inherent understanding that men were respected, men had more opportunities, men didn't have to prove their worth because of the gender they were assigned at birth, and women were treated as secondary in almost every facet of life.

In many ways, I feel that these facts of life for women still hold true. I have spent a lot of time censoring myself for lots of reasons. As many of us women have. Even as I write this book, I find that I am censoring myself, holding back, and I am done. There is a lot of fear in "being done" because I feel like if I lay it all out there, really get vulnerable, then it is as if I'm bleeding out. I have realized that blood cleanses are good, and as the blood flows, it washes away the mask.

This is messy for me to write.

I am attempting to remove the facade.

And I invite you into the mess.

My intention for this book is to get real, get vulnerable, and share my journey of putting down my long-held belief that to be valued I had to be man-like. In sharing my journey, I hope to help you discover your definition of being a woman, what I call your *strut*. While I hope this book will support you in exploring and creating your own definition of your *strut*, I'll share my current working definition.

The word "strut" has been used in many ways, generally describing a confident way of walking, showing confidence and power. My definition of *strut* takes that initial definition and expands upon it. I believe *strut* means the unique qualities of a woman that allow her to own her power and walk tall in life, both literally and metaphorically. Her *strut* allows her to claim and take up all the space she desires with no apologies, owning her own unique place in the world. Below is what to expect within these pages as I share my journey and break down how to define and ignite your strut.

Part I: Ancestral Strut of the Women Warriors

The power of women is part of our lineage, so the first section of this book provides a brief history of women warriors from the fifth century B.C. I included this in the book because in my own journey of defining who I am as a woman, and claiming my strut, I found that understanding that women have historically been true warriors on the battlefield is empowering. Our history is significant because the power of women has been buried, in many ways, and the more I have unpacked the depths of deception that have taken place over time, the better understanding we can have of who we really are.

Part II: Personal Strut

The meat and potatoes of the book, this section contains a description of my own heritage, with stories of my little dynamo grandmother,

mother, and me. These personal stories and experiences illustrate my personal journey of discovering my own inner strut. And they help to demonstrate that despite the efforts of the patriarchy to dampen women's empowerment and belief systems, being connected to other women can keep you connected to your strut.

Part III: The Dream Strut

This section holds stories of the realization of my dream to become a police officer and all that entailed.

PART I:

WARRIOR WOMAN ANCESTRY

WARRIOR WOMAN ANCESTRY:

The Ancestral OG Strut

P art of the reason I believe women do not let their inner strut come through is because of stereotypes and cultural ideals about what defines a woman, what a woman should look like, how a woman should act, and so on. I, of course, have my own experiences and familial history that have shaped my journey in finding my own strut, though it has not always been easy to let that inner wisdom and strength out. So while writing this book, I got curious about the true history of women as a part of the human species, and how their roles may have varied over hundreds of years. Here is what I discovered: historically, women are warriors. Our ancestral heritage includes women who fought on the battlefields alongside men. They sustained the same types of injuries from hand-to-hand combat, wielded the same weapons, rode the same horses, and stood and fought to the end alongside the men.

THE EVIDENCE AND THE TRUTH:

Strut Origins and Fabrications

T he stories of the mythological Amazons are just that, myths, but it seems our sisters from long, long ago could both give and take ass whoopings just like men. Archaeologists have discovered evidence of human, female remains as early as the fifth century that indicate women's involvement in warrior behaviors and rankings in their communities. I have known some women in my time who definitely could be categorized as warriors, for they could surely provide a good ass whooping if necessary, and the gender of the person receiving the whooping was insignificant. I want all women to know that, while we should not go looking for trouble, if it comes, we are not automatically the weaker sex; we have been placed into subservience with layers of lies that try to keep us in place, but our place is wherever we want to be. Recent discoveries prove women are not the weaklings we've been told we are.

Burial mounds of Vikings studied in 2017 proved that in the Viking world, women were warriors, and some were of high caliber and authority. They were buried with their weapons, just like men. And they were women. According to Neil Price in *Children of Ash and Elm: A History of the Vikings,* "An osteological study suggested the buried person was actually female, and this was confirmed by genomic analysis in 2017—the deceased carried XX chromosomes."[1]

In Norse mythology, Valkyrie—also spelled "Walkyrie" and in Old Norse "Valkyrja" (meaning "Chooser of the Slain")—were "any of a group of maidens who served the god Odin and were sent by him to the battlefields to choose the slain who were worthy of a place in Valhalla."[2] The true Viking world's Valkyries were portrayed in artwork and oral storytelling as terrifying. Yet when the Christian monks of medieval times began writing about them, they distorted the stories using their own fantasies to paint these women as beautiful, erotic beings. This is early evidence of males subverting images of women to objectify them as sexually tempting and to hide the authentic power of women. When I discovered this, I thought of the pictures of those big-breasted super hero women in graphic novels and the like, created by male fantasies in the twenty-first century. It seems

---

1 Neil S. Price, *The Children of Ash and Elm: A History of the Vikings*, (London: Penguin Books, 2022).

2 *Encyclopedia Britannica*, s.v. "Valkyrie," accessed October 1, 2023. https://www.britannica.com/topic/Valkyrie-Norse-mythology.

they weren't the first males to sexualize women to subvert their strength and power.

It is interesting to consider the sexualization of female Vikings when the culture already held a belief that inside every human resided a being that was female, so the belief was that even the most heroic, ferocious male warrior had a woman inside of him, a real being, not just a spirit. According to Neil Price's book "The *fylgja* was a female spirit—*always* female, even for a man—and accompanied a person everywhere throughout life."[3] Wouldn't that throw a monkey wrench into the psychological discussions around "getting in touch with the feminine side," or the male side? Many times, men say the first phrase in a joking manner or to demoralize another male, and while this is a characteristic of toxic masculinity, it seems ancient people had a more equalized view of genders.

Another fabrication or distortion is illustrated in contemporary representations of Amazonian women warriors portrayed by the comic book character, Wonder Woman. Written in the myths, and later for the movie screen, Wonder Woman is depicted as coming from an island of only women who were somehow all virgins, but were also great archers and horsewomen. The truth is that there actually were Amazon women, but the name was a conflation of the term perpetrated by Greek culture. The word

---

3 Price, *The Children of Ash and Elm*.

"Amazon" has many connotations depending on which scholar is defining the term. If you want to dive deep, I suggest exploring much of the historical information found in Adrienne Mayor's book *The Amazons: Lives and Legends of Warrior Women across the Ancient World.* What's more important than the term used to describe these women are the archaeological facts that support that women warriors fought in several tribes from Eurasia and the Steppes in ancient times, around the fifth century B.C. The evidence showed women with injuries sustained on the battlefield just like men. The skeletons had evidence of knife wounds and broken bones of the left arm, traditionally the arm holding a shield to block blows in hand-to-hand combat. Women warriors were members of tribes in which, evidently, their men fought alongside them and honored them in burials as their equals, with their weapons, horses, regalia, and even their children.

The Vikings and the Amazons of ancient history are not the only female warriors. Women were snipers in WWII for Russia. The most famous female sniper, Lyudmila Pavlichenko, had the nickname, Lady Death. While she was attending university, she volunteered for the infantry in the Red Army and, at first, was encouraged to become a nurse, but she eventually made her way into the army.[4]

4 Suzanne Raga, "Lady Death: Lyudmila Pavlichenko, the Greatest Female Sniper of All Time," Mental Floss, posted December 6, 2018, retrieved October 20, 2019, https://www.mentalfloss.com/article/565151/retrobituaries-lyudmila-pavlichenko.

The most interesting part is that she became a sniper after grabbing the rifle from a fallen comrade and killing two enemy soldiers, thereby proving her worth. She went on to prove herself many times over. Likewise, Lida Bakieva was another famous female sniper in WWII with a recorded seventy-eight kills.[5] These are two of a substantive list of Russian female snipers who support the notion that women, for centuries, have been badass warriors, keeping societies free and safe.

In even more recent history, the Vietnam War had a female sniper and torturer of infamous acclaim. She was known as Apache, and she became a target high on the list for the American troops because of her sadistic ways. She was killed by Carlos Haithcock, the famous American Sniper of the Vietnam era. All in all, the history here supports the fact that women have every capacity to be as heroic, courageous, warlike, cruel, and vicious as men.

So if this is the true history of women, why do fabrications exist? One, they are simply more entertaining. In addition, they diminish the power of the actual history of women. If the real power of women is not recognized, then women can continue to be depicted as subservient and compliant.

Our history is important, and knowing this history of women warriors is important as well. We

---

5 Lyuba Vinogradova, *Avenging Angels: Young Women of the Soviet Union's WWII Sniper Corps* (Londone: MacLehose Press, 2017).

have been brainwashed, oppressed, demoralized, and hoo-doo-ed to believe that we were meant to be subservient to men. That is not true. That is horseshit. We need our daughters to know our legacy. They need to know they have their own power. All they have to do is understand the history of women and believe in themselves.

If we train our daughters to know and believe this, it could change our world. The victimization of women might very well be on its way to disappearing. The reason we were brainwashed and oppressed by the patriarchy is because of fear, fear of our fierceness as warriors.

The Ancestral OG Strut is the fierce warrior that resides inside each of us. That warrior that had been buried, hidden, oppressed, sexually objectified, raped, beaten, ostracized, bullied, pushed down, and forced into servitude under the guise of proper ladylike decorum and religious bullshit. But the Ancestral OG Strut is still there. Some of us are claiming it, and others are becoming aware of the power of womanhood. I encourage each of you to reach down and grab that deeply hidden, still powerful warrior, and strut your identity. Awaken to your heritage. The strut of the warrior women is not necessarily a physical battlefield anymore, but there are still fields of battle we face every day. The Ancestral OG strutting warrior women did what they had to do to survive and thrive. So can we. All we have to do is find our own strut and use it to rise up and be who we were meant to be: powerful women. Use it to show that we will not be subservient, that we have a purpose, and that we have the right to pursue our dreams. And as you embark on this journey with me, strut your shit. It is your right.

PERSONAL STRUT

EARLY YEARS

My dad wanted a son. He never said it or admitted it, but I know he did. I think something deep inside of me knew this despite his affirmations throughout our lives that "he loved his girls." Pretty early on, I tried to be as much of a boy as I could. One of my aunts told my dad at a family gathering when I was around twelve years old that he had tried to make boys out of both my sister and me. While I don't think that is entirely true, I do believe he wanted us to be strong and independent; he had our best interests at heart.

I came into this world early, and a fighter. My mom began hemorrhaging with me when she was seven months along, and in 1961, not a lot of premature babies made it, but I did. I was relatively healthy, despite being premature. Had I made it the full nine months, I probably would've been a big baby. I think my inner strut was asserting itself in the womb.

Mom and Dad married at nineteen, and I came along as a surprise when they were twenty-one years of age. The doctor's advice to them regarding birth control was incorrect, so there I was. My dad, Wendill, the oldest son of a brood of nine, and mom, Sandy, the second-youngest daughter of a brood of ten, were both born in 1940 to poor families, were teenagers in the late 1950s in the era of Elvis Presley and moonshine, and began their marriage poor as hell and in debt.

My parents were raised with discipline based upon shame and corporeal punishment. Those were the times. Children that they were when they married, my parents clung together in that desperate way that fearful people do when faced with the scary obstacles that life sends at everyone. They were married, and they loved each other, yet the love they had, I think, was predicated upon beliefs instilled in them as they were growing up. They were supposed to find the right one and get married. Being poor didn't matter. They had each other. They didn't allow themselves dreams. That would've been impractical and outside of the norms of their socioeconomic class. Get married, propagate, be pragmatic.

These same cultural principles included keeping secrets and putting up a facade. Let no one know the family problems. Let no one know how much financial difficulty your family is experiencing, how much your parents argue, or that Dad drinks too much too often. Let no one know. That was a cardinal sin, and we weren't Catholic.

The secrets and the facade represent the often common, closed, clannish belief system of folks born in the 1940s and earlier in the South and elsewhere. People perpetuated their belief systems, not understanding the damage they were doing to themselves and others. But really, how could they when they were just trying to survive?

I feel the stronghold of my upbringing as it grasps and pulls at me whenever I read or hear someone opening up about their emotions or their struggles. Even though I know that there is value in being vulnerable, there is always a part of me, that judgmental voice in my head, that tells me to keep that shit to myself, don't reveal too much, that I just want sympathy. Brene Brown has studied and written about this kind of shame-culture mindset for years. My family, like Brown's and so many others, kept our secrets to ourselves for fear of being ashamed. Shame is a big obstacle to overcome in recognizing our inner strut because we have been institutionalized to believe that women should be meek and mild, quiet, small, and a host of other stupid ideas. My family didn't really truck with meek and mild, but we kept that trend toward slight rebellion to ourselves. There was a certain mixture of pride and shame in the independence and strength of the women in my family, and my understanding of who I was growing up as a woman was impacted by this constant tug-of-war I sensed from them.

My parents did the absolute best they could. The biggest thing they did was show up for me every day, so in spite of the shame culture, I was able to overcome the limiting beliefs about women in their roles, though it took me a while. Both of my parents had the foundation of grit and toughness that carried them through a lot. Those two characteristics formed a solid base for me as I have navigated the obstacles of gender role restrictions. Because of my mother's independent spirit and my dad's respect for my mother, I moved forward into a belief system that supports the idea that we don't have to be meek and/or mild. We don't have to wear certain clothes. We don't have to be quiet. We don't have to do a damned thing we don't feel comfortable doing. We have the right to do as we please.

MY MIDDLE NAME AND HINTS OF MY INNER STRUT

My full name is Karen Denise Taylor. In French, Denise comes from "Latin Dionysia, feminine form of Dionysius, a male name of Ancient Greek origin indicating 'Dedication to Dionysus.' Dionysus is the mythological Greek god of wine responsible for growth of the vines and the originator of winemaking."[6] I became fascinated when I was a teenager by the origins of my name because it is the feminine of "Dionysius," the name of a Greek god who was male, yet considered effeminate. My tendency to be less feminine than a lot of women strikes me as ironic when I consider the two names. I have often thought it was an interesting parallel with how the god was effeminate and male, while I am not effeminate but female; perhaps this is due in part to both wishing for my dad's attention because

---

6 "Denise," Names.Org, accessed August 16, 2023.https://www.names.org/n/denise/about.

he wanted a son and maybe even the early stirrings of my strut asserting itself.

Another Greek name that fascinated me early on was the name of the Greek goddess Artemis, which has no similarity to my name, yet it has also intrigued me because she represents many characteristics I admire. She was a strong woman, the child of Zeus along with her twin brother, Apollo, and kept her virginity, loved nature, and was a formidable opponent and huntress, while still protecting animals. She chose to remain a virgin to keep her freedom and do as she pleased. I admire and understand that because, historically, once a woman was married or had sex with a man, he held power over her, so Artemis was choosing to live as she pleased without domination. She was my favorite goddess for this very reason. Because of her beauty and stature, she was pursued by many men who usually met a tragic end as a result of their quest.

After discovering the stories of several bold, warrior women, I started to feel a deeper understanding of myself, and my inner strut began to arise. I began to understand an underlying purpose for my thinking and believing the way I did. I felt a sense of camaraderie with my ancient ancestors who kicked butt and took names. I felt somewhat validated in my struggle to overcome patriarchal oppression and incorrect belief systems. I was named to have the strut, and I wanted to claim it.

OBSTACLES FOR MY STRUT:

Beliefs

My family, especially my maternal grandmother, believed that we should be humble and not proud or conceited. One of her expressions she used to say to me was "pretty is as pretty does," when discussing women who were perceived as being confident in their beauty. I think she was trying to teach me that what is inside of a person is more important than their outward beauty and to keep me from becoming vain. This affected me for a long time because I confused confidence with vanity.

Another phrase I heard a great deal in my youth when someone was gossiping about someone was "he/she is stuck on themselves." It was frowned upon for someone to appear overconfident in my circles. Therefore, I am aware that, to some, using a term like *the strut* to represent inner strength and power might appear inappropriate because of negative connotations and names attributed to people who are confident, such as snob, uppity, or bougie. But the way I view the inner strut of women encompasses a different belief system that hasn't been perpetuated by systems of oppression.

The reason for this belief and attitude about self-confidence has long, gnarly tendrils creeping down into the deepest roots of economic, societal, and patriarchal oppression. The reach of this oppression is so monumental, if it were a tree, it would put the California Redwoods to shame in height and girth. Keeping the oppressed groups humble maintains the status quo, and Southerners, particularly women, still carry the weight of the idea of humility and smallness in order to be perceived as a proper lady.

Much has changed in our culture from my formative years. These days, more people are encouraged to have self-confidence. Many self-help books and speakers promote self-love, for if we can't love the human that inhabits our bodies, it is unlikely that we can truly experience love with another. However, I have come to learn that self-love is important in recognizing our strut. "Conceit" and "confidence" are totally different words with completely different meanings and connotations.

MY PERSONAL ANCESTRAL OG STRUT:

My Maternal Grandmother

> "Women can be found on this island who are far superior in courage and virtue to others of their sex. The historians of the island refer to one Dian-Rhea, who brought the entire island under her scepter. Dian-Nong, Amboulee's princess gave countless proofs of her bravery and magnanimity. Several times she went to war at his side and saved his life more than once."
>
> —DAVID JONES, *WOMEN WARRIORS: A HISTORY*
> (LINCOLN, NE: POTOMAC BOOKS, 2005)

My grandmother's name was Inez, but her brothers called her Ned. She was five foot three, ninety-eight pounds, and married at sixteen years old because that was the way of things in 1921. She really loved school and attended all of the grades that were offered, which meant that she attended school through seventh grade. There was no high school at the time where she lived, in a small town in Western

North Carolina. Despite ending her formal education in the seventh grade, she loved to read, and one of her favorite authors was Barbara Cartland. She also read the Bible, and I have no idea how many times she read it cover to cover, but it was several. Though she had no formal education outside of the school she attended as long as she could, she was one smart cookie and a heck of a storyteller.

My grandma was fifty-six years old when I was born, and I can remember being about eight or ten years old sitting and listening to her stories for hours, and I would imagine what it was like during the time she grew up. She would tell me how when she was six years old, her mother would stand her on a box at the sink in the kitchen to wash the dishes in soapy water in a tin tub. Once the dishes were done, she would use a broom fashioned from straw, bound together at the top, to scrub the floor with more soapy water, no mop. After scrubbing the floor, she and her mother would sweep the water out of the door into the yard. She helped her mother with the laundry (no machine, by hand) for a family of seven brothers, parents, and herself. The clothes were also washed in a tin tub, rinsed, rung out, and hung up outside to dry. If it was cold weather and the clothes froze, she said it made them softer when they thawed. Ironing the clothes involved an iron made from cast iron, quite heavy, which was heated on the woodstove. Ironing clothes this way would help to dry them if they were still damp. While she was small, wielding an iron made from pure cast iron was no task for weaklings. I still have that iron, and I use it as a doorstop. It would make a great weapon in the event of a home invasion. Despite my grandmother's small stature, she contained a lot of strength and power, both inside and out. When I learned of the true existence of the ancient women warriors, I visualized her as one of them. Though she wouldn't have thought of it this way, she had her own inner strut built through tough times. She did what she had to do when she had to do it, and she learned how to be strong in her childhood.

> "History ... demonstrates that the warrior's mantle is a woman's birthright as surely as it is a man's and that the hand that rocks the cradle can also wield the sword."
> —DAVID JONES, *WOMEN WARRIORS: A HISTORY*

Grandma's inner strut was built upon her tough upbringing. In addition to doing the dishes and laundry, she had other duties as a child, like helping in the garden. She told me how she begged her mother to allow her to wear overalls like her brothers when working in the field, but her mother would not allow it, so my grandmother sneaked a pair out of the house, slipped them on to work, and took them off when she was done so her mother wouldn't know. I think part of the reason no one ever sees me in a dress may have something to do with this. Maybe it is my way of pushing back against the patriarchal bullshit she had to endure. I was happy to find that the Amazons wore breeches, something akin to leggings, and armor.

I would like to think that I received a love for storytelling from my grandmother as well. She could surely tell some good stories. It is sometimes hard to wrap my head around everything she had to do to keep her family going, especially after my grandfather died, and she did it all wearing a dress. That may sound trivial to some, but to me, that is a big deal. I am glad that by the time I began attending school in junior high, girls wore pants more, although I do remember more than one teacher saying she wished girls would wear dresses instead of pants. Looking back, I know that was their belief about the roles of women, though they didn't realize they were supporting a custom instilled by a patriarchal society, men who were afraid that if women wore pants, they would step outside the box created for them. Fear is the driving force behind all oppression. Making sure that women weren't allowed to "wear the pants in the family" was a means of keeping them in their places, at home taking care of babies and catering to their husbands and fathers, a form of indentured slavery for many. Wearing skirts and dresses had many purposes, and sexual access was one of them. It is much easier to lift a woman's skirt for quick access than to peel off a pair of pants. Clearly the patriarchy and oppression are self-serving.

SINGLE MOM VS. PEEPING TOM:

A Warrior Protects Her Family

My little grandma, this petite dynamo, birthed ten children of her own, and lost her husband to an aneurysm at thirty-five, with the last few children still at home. She was a single mother in a time when there were far fewer options and resources than today for single moms.

Warriors have to be smart, stealthy, and innovative, and my grandmother was just that when it came to protecting her family. The last four girls were all still living at home, along with my uncle who worked the night shift. The girls were still in school and worked part-time jobs. It was in the early 1950s. By this time, they were living in a rental house with a bathroom. My grandmother never owned her own home. One day, my grandmother noticed a set of footprints outside the bathroom window of the house, and a couple of wooden boxes stacked against the wall that were normally stored in the building at the back of the house. The items were under the bathroom window amongst the shrubs. My grandma deduced they had a Peeping Tom standing on the boxes to look into the bathroom window.

My little grandma got some thin wire and ran it around the shrubs surrounding the house at the bathroom window. She wound it around and around, finally running it in through her own bedroom window, and tied it off around the iron bedpost of her bed. The wire was thin and virtually invisible in the dark, and the distance wasn't far because it was a small house.

That evening, after she had lain down for the night and my aunt, who was the oldest of the three girls, was finishing up in the bathroom, they all heard a loud commotion outside. At the same time as the noise, my grandmother's bed was violently jerked and rapidly slid across the floor toward the window.

She got up and looked outside to see a man trying to fight his way out of the entanglement of wire in the bushes. He got loose and ran off into the woods behind the house. They never had any more problems from creepy assholes peeking in windows.

The most important thing to me about this story is that my little grandma took care of things herself. She didn't try to find a man to help. It was evening, and my uncle was at work. She just used her brain and set a trap. She did what she had to do, and it worked. She knew how to use her intelligence, but she wasn't afraid to stand up to people and beliefs to protect her family. I often wondered what she was planning to do if the guy hadn't run away. I am sure she had a plan, maybe a cast iron skillet upside the head or an iron made from the same stuff. Maybe she would've hit him with an ashtray. Who knows? What I do know is that she wouldn't have cowered in a corner. She was my own personal ancestral woman warrior. She had the strut.

THE WRATH OF A PETITE DYNAMO:

Small Frame, Big Strut

After my grandfather's death and my uncle and two of the four girls got married and moved out, another event occurred that would become one of my favorite stories about my grandmother. My mother told me this tale, and I think the reason my grandma didn't include it in her stories to me was due to her humble nature. She handled her business. She released her inner strut. Done and done.

This demonstration of my grandmother's ire and frustration over shiftless, irresponsible men occurred when my mother was fifteen years old or so, her older sister was eighteen, and the youngest sister was thirteen. The aunt who had been the victim of the peeping tom had moved out. The oldest of the last three had quit school and gotten married at sixteen, after her husband had served in the navy. My grandmother never liked him, and there were good reasons for this. My aunt's husband disappeared at some point after my aunt was pregnant with their second son, and the first was still in diapers. She had to call my grandmother for help because the power had been cut off, and they had no food and no way to get any. In those days, around 1954, it wasn't so easy for women to get jobs, and if they did, there weren't any daycare centers. So my aunt was at home, pregnant, still had one in diapers, and she was in trouble.

My grandmother had always been poor, so it isn't like she had the money to support another family, but she scraped together enough money to buy food and supplies for my aunt and her family and brought them home with her.

The baby was three months old when my aunt's husband showed up drunk at my grandmother's door. My grandmother abhorred alcohol and viewed drinking as one of the worst sins anyone could commit, so this guy already had several strikes against him.

He came to her screen door and wanted to see my aunt. When my grandmother refused, he had the drunken gall to say, "Mrs. Carpenter, you're not being fair."

This was the match that sparked the raging inferno inside of my little grandma. She responded by saying, "Not being fair?" which she punctuated by shoving the screen door open and right into his face, specifically in the center of his forehead. This knocked him backward; he fell down the concrete steps, landing in the yard. My little grandma then grabbed a big, glass ashtray. (If you've never seen one of those heavy old ashtrays from the 1940s and '50s, you can't grasp the significance of this. They were heavy.) She threw that ashtray out the door at him like one of the Amazon warriors throwing a spear in ancient history. It struck him right in the center of his back as he was scrambling up, and my mom said he went running down the sidewalk like he had been set on fire, shirttail flapping behind.

I love the story because it makes my mom and me laugh; my mom laughs literally every time she retells that story about grandma. I wasn't there, but I can sure picture my little grandma flinging that big old glass ashtray and hitting my uncle in the back. Here is where all her chores like hauling water and wood, picking up and carrying kids, milking cows, and ironing clothes with that heavy metal iron paid off. She was a credit to the historical ancestry of the women warriors.

THE NECESSITY OF CREATIVITY

There is an adage I've heard and read many times that goes, "Necessity is the mother of invention," and my grandmother definitely had to be creative in providing for her family. She made my mom and her two sisters' clothes. She couldn't afford much, so she drew her own patterns from newspapers and bought remnants from the fabric shop to make the clothes. She sewed underwear for all of them from bleached and softened flour sacks. Mom said the clothes were always so pretty and so well sewn that they never looked homemade. Grandma could crochet and tat lace as well. She taught me to crochet after I was old enough and wanted to learn, after receiving things she crocheted for me, like hats and purses in all colors and designs, afghans, and many other items. She made them from her own brain because she told me she couldn't use a written pattern for crochet. This is probably because of the necessity of having to create her own patterns, etc., so she had done this for so long, following a pattern was counterintuitive.

UNTIL I GET TIRED:

Warrior Wisdom

The obvious result of having ten children is having grandchildren, and another one of my favorite stories about my grandmother involves my cousins. The aunt with the drunken husband in the ashtray incident ended up having three sons. I will never truly understand why my favorite aunt, with her beautiful soul, stayed with that lout. She had the best heart in the world.

One day my grandmother was watching the boys. The boys were about eighteen months apart in age, and not yet in their teens. The middle and youngest boys would fight sometimes, as kids will do. The oldest was the most like his mother, easygoing and kindhearted, so he never fought. His father called him a coward, but he wasn't. He just didn't enjoy pounding on his brothers.

On this particular day, the two boys were in the yard fighting, so my grandmother picked up her broom and walked outside. My little five foot three, ninety-eight-pound grandma walked up to just a few feet from where they were fighting and waited. Once they had started slowing down a bit, she spoke up and said, "Don't stop. You two just keep on fighting until I tell you to stop," wielding the broom. I visualize a woman warrior swinging her sword in the air as she gesticulates her intention for the boys to continue their foolishness. She made those two boys fight until they were too tired to continue. In my mind's eye, I can see them heaving and falling onto the ground from fatigue.

Now some may think this was hard or cruel, especially in today's world, but consider the time period this occurred. Things were quite different then, and the boys weren't adults. My grandmother wanted them to understand that she was tired of their fighting, so in her way, she was teaching them a lesson on how stupid it was to fight, and at the same time, she was making them tired of it, so that the chances of it happening again would be reduced, at least while she was watching them.

My cousins' father, the same one who left my aunt to have the second child alone and the first one in diapers with no means of support, finally returned home to be a father. One of his parenting techniques was to make the boys fight each other. The oldest didn't like fighting, so the other two would step up and tell their dad they would fight each other instead. So it is understandable on some level why the two boys would fight. It is also important to understand that this kind of thing was acceptable behavior in that time period for some folks. It was considered the art of "making men" out of boys. Of course, we know that it is a load of horseshit, and these days it is called toxic masculinity, but it happened a great deal in those days. Men fighting was accepted and heralded. For example, when the youngest of my three cousins was in high school, a kid called him a son of a bitch. He punched the kid's lights out. In those days, and particularly in the South, calling a guy a son of a bitch was a direct insult to that guy's mother, and it wasn't tolerated. My cousin was suspended, and he had to attend a hearing in front of the school board. Well, to everyone's surprise, his dad, who had failed as a father in so many respects, attended the hearing with my cousin. When the charge was read, my uncle stood up and said, "If he hadn't punched him for saying that, I would've beat his ass." Those were the times, such as they were.

The strange part about this uncle who taught his sons to fight is that he always respected my grandma, even though she hit him with an ashtray. I think he knew she was a tough little nut who had to do what she had to do, but still maintained her virtue. Maybe he saw something deep within her that he was unable to identify. Maybe he saw the warrior within, her inner strut.

POOL HALLS
AND OBLIGATIONS:

A Warrior Doesn't Honor Irresponsibility

This same uncle, after he had returned home and was supposed to be supporting his family, was hanging out in the local pool hall instead of working, and my grandmother found out. I keep writing of her petite size because it is still so hard for me to imagine that little woman doing some of the things she did. She never learned to drive, so she called my dad to take her to the pool hall downtown. I wasn't born yet, so he and mom hadn't been married too long. My grandmother always liked my dad. He treated her with the utmost respect, and if she needed anything, she knew all she had to do was to let him know.

When my dad parked outside the pool hall, she asked him to go inside and get my uncle and bring him to her. Under no circumstance would she have gone inside a place like that. She was a respectable lady, and respectable ladies did not enter pool halls. My uncle had served in the navy and had done some boxing, which may explain his approach to having his sons fight each other. My dad grew up in the country, helping on the farm. When he was in school during recess, he and his friends would fistfight as recreation. This pool hall situation could have resulted in a fight, but for some reason, my uncle walked outside with my dad, without incident, onto the sidewalk where my little grandmother waited. I would have loved to have been a fly on the wall to hear what my dad said to my uncle before they walked outside, but I will never know because dad wouldn't talk about things like that.

My dad must have told my mom about what happened at the pool hall, and later, she told me about my fiery little grandma. Little Ned shook her finger under my uncle's nose and gave him a good dressing down. She told him that a man with a wife and three children should be out working a job instead of hanging out in a pool room. I don't know what else she said, but I know that he stood and took it, and never talked back to her. My mom believes he was afraid of my grandmother, plus my dad was standing there beside her the entire time. I think it was probably a bit of both. It makes people think twice, or at least it did in those days, when a little woman like that is fired up enough to cut loose on someone like that. She was really something else, and obviously, she had her own inner strut that surfaced when she was mad. It also bears mentioning that my dad wasn't afraid of much, so I suspect my uncle didn't want to try that situation out either.

Grandma went about her daily chores and did what she had to do. She never would've thought for a moment that she should be hailed for being a warrior or complimented on having a strut. She just handled her business. My grandmother's stories are so important to me, and I think women need to hear them because we need to know about the ordinary women whom no one ever heard of who fought and protected themselves and their families. We need these true stories to help us stand up for ourselves. We need to understand the shit our female ancestors navigated, so we can face the challenges we must face every day with strength and resilience. We need to understand our worth, pursue our dreams, live our lives, laugh, dance, sing, create, and just live without boundaries or restrictions. We need to claim our struts.

MY PARENTS AND THEIR INFLUENCE ON MY STRUT

Wendill and Sandy were a unit. It doesn't matter their secrets or problems; they stayed together until my dad died. That is an accomplishment that is rare, and it takes resilience. Their marriage had some fairytale-like characteristics along with the normal struggles of any couple. My mom treated my dad like a hero, and my dad treated my mother with respect and honor. They had their faults like anyone else, but they loved each other. There is absolutely no doubt of that. I like to imagine our ancient warrior sisters sharing a relationship with a man with equal respect, both partners heroes in each other's eyes. That is sort of how my mom and dad were.

I used to love it when they would turn on some music and dance in the den. They would also wrestle on the floor, and although my mom was much smaller than my dad, her spirit never gave in. She had that inner strut. She and my dad could be hilariously funny, and despite the problems we experienced as a family, they were there for us, and we knew it. That is the single most important thing, and it is a trait that many, many people did not have in their own lives, and for that, I am extremely grateful.

My dad drove stock cars on dirt tracks when I was just a little kid. I remember standing on the back of a pickup truck in the infield with my mom, aunts, and others, on a Saturday night, watching and looking for his car racing around the curve. I remember once, quite vividly, though I couldn't have been more than two or three years old, looking hard to see him through the open window of his car. I saw his helmet and his arm as he skillfully maneuvered his race car around that track. I thought my dad was the bravest, strongest man on earth. I was so in awe of him, and I loved him so much. So many times in my young life, I wished I had been born male, just so I could be like my dad. Hence my life-long struggle with creating my understanding of self—that warrior-like inner strut I wanted to build—yet often only having male models of success and value, like those I saw in my dad. I didn't know that women could be valuable, successful warriors. I wouldn't learn that until far later in life.

To be fair, mom was no slouch at driving either. On the nights we went to the track to watch my dad race, we would arrive well after him, of course, because he had to haul the race car from the service station that sponsored his car. Once, I remember the track was pretty muddy, and when mom started across it to go to the infield, we started slipping and sliding. I thought it was fun as hell, but mom got a little concerned. No worries though. She just drove that blue Oldsmobile right across that slippery slope down to where dad's truck was parked, and we climbed on the back to get ready to watch.

My dad not only could drive a car like crazy but also was a mechanic. He built an engine and welded a frame to build a go-kart. I was only six or seven, so in order for me to drive it safely, he tied the steering wheel off so that the go-kart was perfectly lined up to go around two trees spaced several feet apart in our backyard. As I got older, he took the rope off, and I could drive the cart without help. I loved that. I would imagine that I was like him, racing stock cars on dirt tracks. Later in life, I would beat my first husband every time he wanted to go somewhere and race go-karts. It drove him crazy that I could beat him at it.

When I was in high school, Mom and Dad bought a silver Chevelle Super Sport. Mom got quite the reputation driving that car. Here was this "proper" lady who would burn the damned tires off that thing at red lights when people challenged her. She was and still is a pistol. I still love that about her. She could also drive my dad's red 1940 Ford truck, with the stick shift in the floor, like nobody's business. My dad told the guys at work that he could park whatever he wanted to in the yard, and Sandy would drive it, no matter if it was a bulldozer. She perpetuated those strut genes my grandma gave her. My mother, like my grandmother, was boxed in by the patriarchy, and I watched them find ways to buck the system. I took note of the bucking to help me build my strut. Driving that go-kart and having a fearless mom helped me many years later; when I became a police officer and attended the police academy, I would exhibit my genetics on the driving course and cause my instructor, a state trooper, to chuckle, shake his head, and just say, "I love it." That was the most the man had said the entire time. I have some of my dad's traits and some of my mom's, but to be fair, I have developed many bad habits that can't be attributed to anyone but myself. My sense of honor and pride were cultivated by my upbringing that has tracked down through generations; much of that constituted a foundation of strength and resilience.

I HAVE A BIG CHIP ON MY SHOULDER

'm not going to remove it. In fact, I think we need more women with chips, so we can set things right

As I got older, I struggled with trying to understand why the men and boys got all of the breaks. As a result, over time, I began carrying a big chip on my shoulder. This chip carried me through some things, and it caused me problems too, especially in relationships with men. These problems began early on.

When I was in the fifth grade, I had a kid say that he was going to call me "Joe," after the famous football quarterback Joe Namath, because I was bigger than all of the girls my age and many of the boys. I was also overweight, so that little nickname held a lot of pain for me that I squashed and never shared with anyone in an attempt not to be victimized any more. Instead of acting like the nickname hurt, I acted like it was a compliment and tried even harder to be a boy as much as I could. I was young and didn't get the difference and freedoms between boys and girls, but I also wanted to fit in, like any other fifth grade kid in the world. I wasn't petite and cute like the other girls. I was heavier with glasses, braces, and unruly hair, and I liked to beat the boys at games we played. In those days, it wasn't common at all for girls to want to beat the boys at anything, and I was targeted for my looks, especially my weight. But something inside of me recognized there was more spurring me on, other than just the name-calling I was getting around my weight and looks. My budding inner strut was starting to ignite. While it took many years for me to recognize this, I now see how that desire to be seen for who I was and the unique strengths I had was there all along. One benefit I did enjoy from the advantage of my size and attitude was being picked early on for softball games. My dad taught me how to hit, catch, and throw, and I was good at it.

Adolescence is difficult in any era, but in mine, the 1970s, bullying went on, and no one did anything about it. We just had to learn how to cope the best way we could, so my way of handling being overweight and larger in stature than most kids my age was to be as boyish as I could within the limits my mother would allow. I often wonder if I had been born in the days of the women warriors, would I have been respected for my size instead of denigrated for it?

I was pretty shy as a kid. It took me quite a few years to get over that, but I did. I guess I got tired of being pushed around and made fun of. Because of my size, I had girls try to pick fights with me in school, but I never fought. I had a very healthy fear of getting in trouble in school because I knew my dad would whip my ass. Also, my mom pounded into our brains her belief that "only White trash fight." That goes back to that ever-present belief system of chasing respectability, so that no one could call us White trash.

Being overweight and larger than all the other kids my age not only made me a target for ridicule and girls wanting to fight but also carried with it the problems of buying clothes that would fit, and rarely did I have anything deemed proper attire for girls that was comfortable. Both of my parents believed in wearing appropriate clothing for the circumstances, so of course, I was forced to wear dresses. After I reached middle school, I wore pants more, but no blue jeans until high school. Shorts weren't allowed to be worn to school by anyone, boys or girls, except in physical education class. In gym class, we weren't allowed to wear t-shirts; we had to wear white, button-up blouses and black or red shorts that were no shorter than the tips of our fingers with arms hanging at our sides. It was hard to find a button up blouse that fit me and didn't pull between the buttons, not so much because of a large stomach, but because I grew boobs early. I still don't get why we couldn't wear t-shirts.

What we wore, how we behaved, how we walked, and how we talked were all regulated by the "establishment," to use a '60s term, and this only added to the ever-growing chip. At the time, I didn't know much about feminist ideas, but I remember hearing about women burning their bras when I was in my preteens. At that age, I didn't think about that a lot, but I remember my mother thinking that act was just scandalous. Maybe it was to her and many like her, but later on, I understood the symbolism of it. I got it, and after I began the research for this book, I thought about our ancestors and how they performed their duties, whether fighting, training, or just doing chores, without bras. Hell, they probably didn't have underwear either.

In my younger teenaged years, somewhere deep inside, I started thinking, "This is not fucking fair. If I want to do whatever, I should be able to, regardless of my gender." Growing up, I always wanted to be a boy because I could see they had more opportunities than I did, and my notice of this fostered unfairness grew as I got older; maybe it was my purpose to come into this life and say, "Hell no. That's not right. I'm not putting up with that shit." Looking back, this is when my inner strut began to assert itself and eventually fed the dream of becoming a cop.

PART III:

THE DREAM STRUT

BEFORE THE DREAM CAME TRUE:

The Strut Emerges

Because the required exam for the police department stipulated that applicants must be twenty-one years old to sit the test, I got a job doing security work at a hospital to have a decent salary and benefits while I waited for my twenty-first birthday. One weekend, my friends and I decided to go to the movies. We never made it.

Though I've experienced more than one brush with death in my lifetime, one incident is particularly significant. I was to turn twenty-one in a couple of weeks. As my two friends and I were on our way to the movies, a woman in a Honda Civic ran a stop sign, smashed into us, and totaled my car and hers. The collision threw my friend sitting in the front seat out onto the ground and my friend sitting in the back seat down in the floorboard, while the metal horn from my 1966 Ford Mustang detached from the steering wheel and went through my face as my head hit the steering wheel, breaking my upper and lower jaws, taking several of my teeth with it.

My jaws were wired for six weeks, and I was on a liquid diet. That was the least of the problems. Because the driver of the other vehicle and her passenger died, lawyers became involved. I was not at fault. I was not speeding. I had violated no traffic laws. I was just a twenty-year-old kid on her way to the movies with friends and even looking forward to her twenty-first birthday coming in a few weeks, complete with a planned trip to the Bob Seger concert for which her friend had bought tickets as a birthday present. Bob Seger was my favorite artist.

By all accounts, I could've died that day, but I didn't. I took a hell of a hard lick to the head, but we've always joked about how hardheaded I am. To this day, I remember nothing about the moments on the road just before the accident. What I know now, I learned after the fact. I only remember waking up and lifting my head from the steering wheel, dazed. I remember touching my face because it felt weird, and I realized I had no feeling in my lower lip, but I could feel with my hand that I had way more lip hanging than I should. Even more disturbing was my bottom teeth laying back and down against my tongue.

I looked down, and my chest was bloody. I looked to the passenger seat, but my friend wasn't there. As I was turning my head, trying to get my bearings, the car door opened, and an arm reached in to help me out. A lady helped me from the car and guided me to the curb to sit down. To this day I have no idea who that lady was.

Emergency response procedures dictate that she should've left me alone until the EMTs and paramedics could get a C-collar on me and put me on a backboard because of the nature of the injury, but I have never blamed her. She was only trying to help, and though it could've ended in death or paralysis, it didn't. I sat on the curb while they loaded my friend on a stretcher into the ambulance. Apparently, she had been thrown through the window, breaking her leg and causing some other injuries.

I climbed into the ambulance myself and sat on the seat in the back as they transported us to the emergency room. Bad day. I remember lying on a stretcher in the emergency room hearing my mother's voice when they tried to tell her that only one person per patient was allowed in the back. I heard her all the way back where I was. She was scared, and I knew it, but I knew my little mama was on the way. I heard, "That's her DADDY!" Mama, the ultimate lady, no longer cared what anyone thought. She was on the way to her child, and her husband was coming with her. That was that. That warrior woman ancestry came through in a big way, and Mom showed her strut.

Now Dad was a big guy. He sported an eighteen-inch neck and had forearms bigger and more muscular that a lot of guys' biceps, but he was quiet, and I suspect that, had mom not addressed the rule of only one person at a time visiting with a patient, he probably would have just looked at them, scared the bejesus out of them, and come on back. At any rate, they were allowed back to my room, which technically wasn't a room. It was a space with equipment, a stretcher, a bunch of medical personnel working on me, and curtains, no walls.

I remember some things that happened while I was in that room, but only a little. Once both parents came in to check on things, my dad stayed with me while Mom went outside in the waiting room. She did that, I know, because she was so distraught over the state of my face, I am sure. She couldn't bear that I was hurt that badly, and I know she was afraid. I am sure my dad was too, but he was the one who was steady in emergency situations, and she accepted that. She knew her abilities, and she knew her limitations. She and my dad worked well together because they each knew these things about one another.

The first night in the hospital room, my dad stood over me all night. I was kind of out of it due to the medications, and surgery was scheduled for the next day, but I was in and out. Because of the trauma to my head and teeth, I had trouble with blood choking me, and periodically, I would need suction so that I could breathe. My dad, always stalwart, never easily shaken, watched over me like a hawk. I do remember hearing panic in his voice once. I was gagging from the blood, and he must have pushed the nurse's button more than once because a voice from the nurse's station came over the intercom, and she was rude. My dad said, "She's choking. Get in here!" It didn't take long for a nurse to appear and run the suction. The thing was, if they would've left the suction, my dad was the type to do it himself. Over the years, I have buried a lot of memories, but I have never forgotten the panic I heard in my dad's voice that night because I never heard that type of reaction out of my dad before or after. I did see his face turn pale the night I walked in from work with my arm in a sling and dirt all over me, but that is another story; I will get to it in the *Being a Cop and Having a Life: Strut Contradictions* chapter. I still have a steel pin in my jaw from the surgery that put the mandible and maxilla back together. After my parents had spent scads of money on braces for me, of the very teeth that were straightened and had only been free of braces for a short period of time, several were broken out of my mouth, never to return. In addition, after seven hours in surgery putting my face back together, my mom and I were in the hospital room when an insurance agent came in asking us to sign a waiver, so he could do a blood test on me for drugs. I was a rules-abiding teenager who had never even had a taste of alcohol, and hearing that while laid up in a hospital bed with both jaws wired really got to me. My mom was not happy. That insurance agent fired up my mom's inner strut.

Always the "proper" lady, mom just took the paper and laid it to the side and told him she would look at it. He tried to persuade her to sign it, but my mom gave him a look that would melt ice in the North Pole, and he shut up and left. When he left, I started crying. Now, my mom wasn't through with him, but she wasn't going to upset me because of what I had just gone through. She told me not to worry about it, but I knew she was mad, and I had an idea that guy was about to find out just how inappropriate his behavior had been.

She left me and went on to work that day, and I found out later that she went straight to her desk, picked up the phone, and called that agent. I don't know what all she said, but I know she told his ass off without using the first curse word. That is my fiery little mama, a member of the OG Strut Club. I have always respected the way my mom could tell someone off in no uncertain terms and never curse. That is not me, but I am good with that. I have to be who I am, and my mom has always been more sheltered from certain aspects of the world than I have.

During the six weeks my jaws were wired, my mom, who only weighed 125 pounds at five foot five inches tall, lost fifteen pounds. She couldn't eat because I couldn't eat anything. Even though I was on a liquid diet, I couldn't even handle milkshakes because they were usually too thick. After several weeks, the swelling in my face went down, and after that came quite a lot of reconstructive dental work. I returned to work after a while and went on with my life, but this incident affected me in a lot of ways. It would have been good to have sought counseling, I am sure, but seeking therapy just wasn't that common in those days.

Ultimately, the fight that brought me into the world early presented itself again as a result of this accident. There were many months of mental rehabilitation that I navigated on my own with some help from my friends and family. I don't remember exactly when I realized that the reason I didn't die that day was because I had a reason to stay. I had to be a warrior to make it through the things that arose from that accident, some of which I still won't talk about. But I know that although it was a rough thing to go through, I am stronger because of it, and I began to feel my warrior roots, my inner strut, though I didn't call it that yet. My strut was growing and strengthening more than ever.

MY DREAM AND THE RISE OF THE STRUT

wanted to be a cop from the time I was around eleven or twelve years old. Of course, people laughed when I told them, so I stopped telling them. Television shows like *Police Woman* with Angie Dickinson in the '70s helped me define my dream, but the plots were rather ridiculous. That was the culture of the time. The fact that the female cop ended up always having to be saved by the men irritated me, even at that age. Later in life, the television show *Hunter* came out, and I liked it a lot better because the character, Dee Dee, was tough and kicked ass, despite her small stature. She exuded confidence and strength like her ancestral sisters, and even though it was fiction, it resonated with me.

It took a few years and a lot of tries before I realized my dream, but when I did, I was stoked. Let me back up here and reset. The city police department only offered the Civil Service Exam and agility course once per year, so the accident took away my chance to try out that year I turned twenty-one, but I placed my application with the county sheriff's department where I lived, passed the tests, got an interview, and I got the job. The problem with the job at the sheriff's department was that I was hired as a dispatcher. The sheriff wanted fully commissioned deputies working in the communications center dispatching his deputies, so that is where women were placed upon hire. This was the 1980s, and there weren't that many women in law enforcement in my town at that time, and of the ones that were, many were relegated to desk jobs and communications.

When I was hired, my dad bought me my service revolver. In those days, the department didn't provide the service weapon for us. That said a lot to me because my dad was not enamored with me becoming a deputy, but I know he was proud, nonetheless.

I worked for the sheriff's department for three or four years. I honestly cannot remember because it has been so long. But I married one of the deputies on the third shift that I dispatched and, a year later, had my son. I left the sheriff's department and tried my hand in the civilian world for a bit, but I was miserable because I hadn't yet achieved my dream of being a real police officer who worked on the street. The only chance I would have to get on patrol was to pass the Civil Service Exam and agility course for the city police department because the chief of the police department was putting women officers on the street.

I finally passed the tests after a couple more tries and achieved my dream of being a cop, a warrior, a protector. My strut was rising. I had hung tough and didn't give up despite having to run the physical agility course a few times before passing. I hadn't trained enough for it during that time because I didn't have the knowledge to properly prepare for it, but I finally did pass. The day I passed, I went and sat in my truck and burst into tears of joy. No one was around but my inner strut, and she gave a war cry, holding her battle ax above her head in victory.

FEMALE COP, PATRIARCHAL CRAP:

Wielding the Strut

In my role as a police officer, I had to learn to navigate patriarchal attitudes in a predominantly male profession. This was in the 1990s, and though there were women cops, there weren't a lot of them, at least not in the department where I worked. To say that teachings from my mother on how to handle unwanted advances from men came in handy would be the understatement of the century. The inappropriate comments and attitudes came not only from some men in the department, but also from men on the street. It was a minefield that we women had to traverse every single shift, no exceptions. One common statement I heard from men on the street was, "Ooh baby, you can handcuff me anytime," or some such nonsense like that. The inner stirrings of my strut were getting stronger as I learned to deal with these incidents. These types of comments are representative of the patriarchal bullshit women must navigate on the daily. Though it has been years since I was a cop, I know women still deal with this kind of thing today.

The background I have in working around a bunch of men salted me up pretty well. I have seen how men behave within a group of guys, how they talk, how they relate to each other, and what they say. There is only so long any of us can put up a facade, so I saw the real deal, and it helped me to understand things about men that women without that advantage sometimes don't know. For example, they could stand around and talk shit about women they saw, how they were dressed, how they acted, how they would like to get into their pants, or how the woman in question was ugly, fat, etc., but let them believe another man was looking at their wife, girlfriend, etc., in the same types of ways, and they would lose their shit. Double-standard, and for sure they didn't even think about that. More than once, I pointed that out to them.

I struggled with reconciling my upbringing regarding being a lady with being a cop on the street. The emphasis on being a lady that I was raised with came into direct conflict with some of the ways I had to navigate my environment as a police officer. I did what I needed to do to assert myself and let my male coworkers know I wasn't going to be dropping my drawers for any of them. My inner strut was getting stronger each time I asserted myself.

During this time, I really began to question this "ladylike" expectation upon which I had been raised and pondered what exactly it meant. I pushed back on the pressure of maintaining that "put her on a pedestal" idea, and it was rather easy to do when I was being exposed to all of the things I faced each shift I worked. I wanted to be treated as an equal and not placed on some imaginary riser, worshiped for my femininity. I wanted to be recognized as a cop, not a female cop. I was stubborn and vocal about being treated differently. The days on the force were fundamental in me starting to recognize my inner strut.

However, I did have to learn how to be more diplomatic when it came to dealing with those who outranked me. There was no #MeToo movement at the time. And although sexual harassment was supposed to be against the rules, if a female reported a male for it, especially one with rank, there was very little, if anything, done to the accused, and the woman was ostracized. Eventually, she would be fired for anything those in charge could come up with, and if they couldn't find something, they would make something up. This wouldn't end with the department. They would blackball the officer, so she wouldn't get a job anywhere else in the county, and usually the state. Police departments are connected in ways many people don't realize, so if this sounds like an exaggeration, it is not.

I had a lieutenant whom I had known for a while because he had been my sergeant before he was promoted. He kept hinting at us getting together. "Getting together" with this tomcat would mean sex, plain and simple. He was divorced, and I was in the middle of a divorce at the time. He already had several girlfriends. In order to keep from making my life hell, I thought a lot about how to handle this guy and finally told him one day that we were just too good of friends to mess it up with an attempt at anything else. I felt he was reasonable enough to accept that, and I was right, but before I walked away, he told me if we were ever to get together, it would be the best I ever had. Geez. I just smiled and walked out. I couldn't say anything else to that, or it would've caused me big trouble, for sure. It worked out though, because he left me alone after that, and we were still able to be friends. My inner strut had allowed me to be strategic in dealing with such a moment *and* to keep a job that I loved. For better or worse, I learned how to navigate men in power over me if I wanted to keep my job. The job was my dream, even with all of the male ego manipulations.

"It was customary for young women to prove themselves in battle, and that older women fought by choice, or whenever necessary."

—ADRIENNE MAYOR, *THE AMAZONS: LIVES AND LEGENDS OF WARRIOR WOMEN ACROSS THE ANCIENT WORLD* (PRINCETON UNIVERSITY PRESS, 2014)

We women had to prove our worth by passing the same tests as men, including written, physical, shooting, and defensive tactics examinations, and graduate from the police academy, etc., but we still had to deal with the sexual innuendos and the tendencies of our male partners and fellow officers who felt they needed to protect us. I once had a partner step between me and a possible suspect when the suspect called me a bitch; I cursed him out after the call was completed. It would've been stupid to show any irritation with my partner in front of a suspect and cause a distraction, but what took the cake was my partner stepping between me and the guy and telling him not to "talk to her like that." I told him I wasn't his wife, girlfriend, or mother and instead of his protection, I just needed his backup like he would any male officer.

Another time, a few months after I had been promoted to narcotics, we were preparing a large drug bust operation. When we planned a big operation, we would bring in extra officers to help us, so the day we hit a drug house on a search warrant, we had some officers with us that day who normally worked patrol. They were in plain clothes instead of uniforms.

Once we entered the house and were executing the search warrant, one of the patrol officers walked up to me and proceeded to give me directions as to what I should make sure I took care of. This guy was a first class ass-kisser for the higher-ups anyway, which made it worse, but he was also a misogynistic jerk. When he started telling me what to do, I pretty much told him to fuck off and mind his own damned business. It has been many years, so the words I used were probably different, but I was loud enough for my sergeant to hear and come over to ask what was going on. This was our female sergeant, so I felt more comfortable telling her why I was so damned pissed off. Nothing was done, of course, but the jerk-off left me alone after that, once he expressed his confusion at why I had told him to fuck off. I don't know if he would ever have gone up to one of my fellow male narcs and done the same thing, but I seriously doubt it. There was no strategic or diplomatic appearance of the strut on this occasion. He pissed me off, and I let him know. My inner strut, that warrior in my spirit, wanted to castrate him on the spot.

Constantly navigating the chauvinistic patriarchy already, once I realized my dream of becoming a police officer, I had to find a way to walk that tightrope between knowing what to ignore and what to address when it came to comments and actions from coworkers and supervisors. I didn't want to be treated any differently because I was a female officer, but that was just a pipe dream. My inner strut built some solid muscle during those years, and now I think about those women warriors and smile because I know that sometimes my ancestry was there, looming in the background, bolstering me up. We women can assert our power loudly when the situation calls for it. We can claim our right to be treated fairly and equally by claiming our inner strut, but we need to do it together like our ancestors on the battlefield.

PROBLEMS FROM THE WOMEN UNAWARE OF THEIR STRUT

The chip on my shoulder wasn't there only because of what men said or did; my perception of experiences with women had a lot to do with it too. Sometimes one woman could make it seem as though the progress we had made as women in a male-dominated role was erased. I remember one new female hire shared that the police department was "a good place to find her next husband." She had a reputation for bursting into tears whenever she became frustrated or failed at a training exercise. Needless to say, she didn't last through all of the training. This type of thing would really send me over the edge. I saw her words and emotions she seemed to express through crying as a means of emotional manipulation. Because I had a very hard view of manipulative people, I saw the actions of this potential female police officer as a step backward in the progress I felt we women had made. As I look back on my upbringing, I can see how my own stories may have unfairly influenced my view of this woman (and sometimes other women).

My father raised my sister and me with no patience when it came to crying. I mean none. There were only certain situations where crying was accepted, and they were few and far between. I can see now, even as I'm writing this, how my father's view of crying, which got passed on to me, is the foundation for the chip on my shoulder. I understand the purpose for my dad not wanting us to cry. He wanted us to "man up." Trust me, I get the irony of the metaphor here, but I believe his approach had to do with him making sure that we could tackle life in a way that said, "Some things are out of our control, so just deal with it and move on." For him, and therefore for me, crying equaled complaining and not dealing with things out of our control. So at the time, in my eyes, if a woman wished to be a cop, she needed to be tough as hell, which meant never crying. Because of my story around tears, I had decided that crying would potentially give men the opportunity to call a woman weak, especially a female police officer. In those days, I was really harsh and unforgiving with any perception of a woman feeding into what I had come to believe were stereotypes for women, like them using emotion to be manipulative. Because of the way I was taught that tears represented manipulation, I still catch myself getting angry if I tear up. My inner voice calls me a weak, emotional woman, but I know this is a very unhealthy attitude. I did my best at the time with what I knew, and I do believe this perspective on crying served me in some way for many years, especially when I was on the force.

Now that I have learned about the women warriors who were our ancestors, I wonder if they cried. I am sure they did, and these women were treated as equals on the battlefield, had babies, and were obviously accepted for their abilities to be both nurturing and powerful, not diminished or placed in a subservient role. I have no proof, but I suspect these women were probably honored and accepted for their abilities, including their emotional abilities, leaving the men to be themselves and not fear the power of women. This fear of women's power is what drives patriarchal oppression.

These are the kinds of things I consider as I learn more about my inner strut. After all, crying is a reaction of human emotion, so the oppressive nature of how I have viewed it is another cultural construct that I am disassembling. Although I once viewed showing emotion as a sign of weakness at best and manipulation at worst, I am learning that it is not. It is human, and my inner strut representative of a warrior will be stronger if I don't suppress emotion. Suppressed emotion is dangerous.

I imagine women warriors on the battlefield and compare that to how I viewed crying as showing weakness. The image of any warrior crying over the loss of a comrade seems acceptable, yet being stoic under that type of circumstance was something I worked hard to do then, and sometimes still. My inner strut is wise and still teaches me things every day, so when I consider my long-held belief that crying is not acceptable in public, I find I have more work to do. Did those women warriors cry when their babies were born? Did they cry when they lost a comrade or a mate on the battlefield or from sickness? It probably depended upon the individual warrior, but I imagine if a woman was fierce in battle and also chose to cry, no one would've had the intestinal fortitude to challenge her and call her weak. I believe our patriarchal culture, developed in different regions than those who had the women warriors, is the culprit behind certain expectations in behavior. Now, the wisdom of my strut advises me, but in the past, I was stoic, fought back tears, and felt fear deep in my gut many times for my comrades.

A COMRADE DOWN:

The Angry Strut

As police officers, we fought on the battlefield everyday, though it wasn't viewed that way. All police officers enter a battlefield of sorts every time they begin a shift. Most of the guys on my platoon when I worked uniform patrol were great guys. Most of them were married with children, and only a couple were dicks, but we looked out for each other, even the ones who were dicks, because that blue uniform held the same meaning as the armor, bows and arrows, battle axes, and swords of an ancient army. Knowing that we all had each others' backs was helpful, and once my guys got to know me, they saw that I would be there. My inner strut gave me the courage to do what I had to do, both alone and with a partner. She was there, strengthening my spirit and bolstering my courage on every call, especially the ones I knew could be more dangerous than others.

There have been several times in my life when, had the timing been a second or two late or early, or had some other small circumstantial detail been different, I would not be sitting here writing this book. One incident that is still pretty vivid in my memory happened when I was working the midnight shift (11 p.m.–7 a.m.), and I was checking buildings in my zone. We were expected to keep an eye on businesses and residential areas for break-ins and such. I was behind a building and saw a car drive into the parking lot of a restaurant one site over. I sat behind the building, waiting to see what happened. Just as I realized it was an early employee coming in to prepare the kitchen for cooking, I got a call on the radio regarding a domestic dispute.

I put the car in park and picked up the radio mic to let dispatch know I was on my way, when unit 14, one of my fellow officers, notified dispatch that he was closer to the call than I was and would take it. Dispatch acknowledged him, so I responded that I would head that way as well. One officer should never respond to a domestic dispute. Those calls have the potential for all kinds of bad things happening and getting out of control because many times, the victim who called will jump to the aid of the abuser if they see the abuser is going to be arrested. At any rate, unit 18 responded to my call and said he was right behind unit 14 and would back him up. So basically, twice, I was called off.

I pulled out into the street and rolled toward my next set of buildings to check. I heard both guys call out on the domestic. It seemed like only about a minute had passed; I hadn't gotten very far along on my building checks when I heard the voice of 18 come on the radio. He was yelling that there was an officer shot. My gut dropped down to my toes and probably added power to the punch I put on that accelerator as I sped toward their location.

Fear for my fellow officer and anger over the situation fueled my drive as much as the gasoline in the cruiser. I went into a deep focus on my driving and getting to those guys as fast as I could. I surmised that it was probably 14 who was shot since 18 made the frantic call. It was a good thing it was the third shift. I didn't have to deal with much traffic on the roads. I cut through the back roads in the mill village, went airborne over the railroad tracks, and found out later I had bent the push bar on the front of the cruiser when I landed on the asphalt road. I did not care. As I squealed into the parking lot of the apartments, the scent of burning rubber filled my nose. It wasn't mine. Several other cruisers were there, and apparently, at least one or two had touched down hard and abused their brakes and tires.

I jumped out and ran to the apartment. Our sergeant was on scene with some of the other guys. As the rest of us arrived, sarge sent us back out on the street to cover calls. They were loading 14 onto the ambulance, 18 was unhurt, which was great. Apparently, the male involved in the encounter, during a wrestling match on the couch, grabbed one of the officer's guns, and it went off and shot 14 in the arm.

This was many, many, years ago. Lots of things have changed since then, including officers being equipped with various nonlethal weapons like tasers, etc. to use in situations like that. We didn't have many of those nonlethal weapons, and the weapons we had weren't appropriate for close-quarters fighting. So when units 14 and 18 engaged their suspect and were trying to subdue him, their options were limited. Despite being under attack from the suspect, the circumstances were such that they couldn't just shoot the guy. That wasn't acceptable under the steps set forth by procedural standards.

Fortunately, 14 recovered and returned to work after a few weeks of rehab. He was always a good guy, and several years after I left the PD, I learned he had made detective. He deserved it.

I have always thought about that night as a close call for me because I was supposed to get that call. I tried to go twice, but both times, I was denied. Without sounding too woo-woo about it, I think there were invisible forces working that night; maybe my inner strut really is the spirit of some ancient warrior. Otherwise, I have no logical explanation for why 14, not me, ended up being the one who responded to the call and was shot.

Just like my premature birth and the tragic car accident, once again, it seemed I had made it through a perilous situation. I had been spared probably serious injury or death. It didn't take me as long to understand this as it did after my car accident. Either I was either really lucky, or I was definitely supposed to be here. I don't believe in luck, so I knew that there was a certain thing or things, purpose or purposes that I needed to complete while here in the physical plane. I wasn't sure if it was being a cop, a mother, a wife, a daughter, or more, but I knew there was a definitive reason. Though I didn't realize it at the time, my inner strut was building momentum, and those women warriors in my ancestry were in the background fighting for my survival. Maybe the reason I was spared was so I could write this book and get the message out that women are warriors, to help my sisters recognize and embody their strut.

BEING A COP AND HAVING A LIFE:

Strut Contradictions

I married when I was twenty-six, and that marriage ended in a divorce seven years after I realized my dream and became a cop at the age of thirty-four. My first husband had a lot of immaturity and anger issues, and I was glad when the marriage ended. I did not remarry until after I had been a police officer for a few years, and my son was seven years old. My second marriage was to a fine Southern man, Billy, and though he has been gone seventeen years now, I miss him every day.

The funniest story about Billy and me getting married is one involving my best friend. I had been legally separated for a year and hadn't dated anyone. I was raising my son, working as a cop, and navigating the issues my ex was causing me, but I was doing okay. After my shift, I would park the cruiser in the back lot and walk past the fire department on my way to the squad room. A few of the firemen would sometimes be out back behind the station, and we would strike up a conversation. I didn't know Billy when I first started stopping to chat, but after a couple of weeks of talking, one day he asked me on a date. I said okay. The funny part happened when I told my best friend, Margaret, about it. I told her I had changed my mind and was going to tell Billy I decided not to go out with him. She and I were both going through divorces, but she didn't have children. I will never forget it. She said, "Oh good grief. Go out on the date, girl. It's not like you're going to marry him." We joked for years about how she "jinxed" me with that comment.

Billy was like most Southern men and, as such, believed it was his job to protect me, even though I was the cop. Again, it was that patriarchal belief that women need to be protected. I had to tap into my inner strut to get Billy to understand that I didn't need protection. He got better, but he never truly stopped. While we were dating, I had an incident occur on duty that ended in me getting injured. When Billy found out, he was furious, and I know part of it was because it scared him, but also, part of it was because it had happened when he was away fishing and unable to (in his mind) protect me. Of course, had he been at home, he couldn't have protected me then either, but emotions are sometimes irrational.

While Billy was fishing with friends in Destin, Florida, for a week, I was working one afternoon when

I heard a call dispatched for unit 15 to go check out a possible drug-related call. The dispatcher sent no backup with the responding unit, and there were reportedly three suspects hanging around a residence in a government apartment complex. Though I was across town, I keyed the mic and told them I would back the officer up because no cop should be dispatched on a call in which they're outnumbered.

When I arrived at the apartment complex, the young rookie officer was talking with some fellows who were hanging around in front of the apartment buildings. This was government-sponsored housing for low-income families, and rules were in place in those apartment complexes that were specific in regard to illegal activities. When we ran checks on the guys, one of them came back with a trespass notice for that complex, and he was in violation.

We walked him to my patrol car, and I had him lean against the car so that I could pat him down for weapons and arrest him. I made a big mistake by not cuffing him before I patted him down for weapons. It was my fault for not following good protection procedures. When I reached to check the waistband of his pants, he spun around on me, and the fight was on. Had I cuffed him first, the fight wouldn't have gotten out of control like it did. My fault, plain and simple.

We were fighting with this guy, and the rookie officer hadn't been on the street long, only a few weeks. This young officer topped out at around 125 pounds soaking wet with rocks in both pockets. We fought the assailant for what felt like a long time. In reality, it was probably only a couple of minutes, but when you're fighting, a couple of minutes is a long time. By the time we got him restrained, but not in handcuffs yet, we were surrounded by a large group of people from the apartment complex who had encircled us, yelling and raising hell. A guy ran up and asked if I needed help because I had my suspect in front of me, holding him against me by his chest, and my rookie partner had locked both arms around the suspect's legs, and I was basically dragging him and the suspect backward away from the crowd. The main thing I was thinking about was keeping my right elbow locked down on my pistol because I promised myself I wasn't going to be killed with my own gun. When the guy tried to help, three guys from the crowd stepped up and pushed the guy away.

Never in my career had I ever used the universal code for "officer in trouble" until that day. I keyed my walkie mic and said, "Unit 19, double zero." No one knows what that is like unless they have lived it. Even as I wrote that, I got goosebumps. Once I did that, it sounded like Armageddon. Sirens from all over the city and county lit up, and I knew the calvary was on the way, if I could just hold on.

Only cops can understand the feeling that washes over you when you hear all that help headed your way. The responding officers feel it too, in a different way. Adrenaline floods the veins, heart rates increase, and fear for the fellow officer in trouble enters your consciousness. I didn't even know half the officers who showed up, but they were my brothers and sisters, and I knew I would make it.

Unfortunately, when the three guys from the crowd intervened, I lost my grip on my suspect, and he ran. My partner was trying to hold on, but he got hurt. I was so damned mad at those guys causing me to lose my suspect that I waded up into the dispersing crowd yelling, "Where are those bastards?" I wanted those assholes who had helped my suspect. I wanted them bad, but once those sirens lit up, the crowd dispersed faster than you can believe. The three guys disappeared, and so had my suspect. I was really angry. No one had ever seen me that angry.

Everyone came, the county sheriff's department, all the guys from my department—hell I think I even remember a state trooper there. My chief showed up along with my lieutenant, sergeant, etc. My shirt was dirty and torn; my left wrist was rapidly swelling from bracing myself as I fell and caught myself on the sidewalk while ducking a punch. The duck out worked; he never connected, but I had gotten a good side kick in.

My supervisors were standing there talking with me while the rest of the blue brotherhood finished dispersing the crowd and some EMTs loaded my partner up in an ambulance. My sergeant saw my wrist and said I needed to go have it looked at.

I was mad. I had fire in my eyes. My inner strut rose up and really showed out that day. I looked at my sergeant, and I said, "I'm not giving these assholes the satisfaction of seeing me ride in the back of an ambulance. Fuck that." I said it right in front of the brand new chief and didn't give a damn. My sergeant looked at one of my fellow officers and a good friend of mine and told him to take me to the company doctor in the cruiser. My inner strut was still being unleashed. My inner warrior was angry because I had lost my suspect, and I knew there would be those who would say that it happened because I was a woman. I fought like hell and lost control of my suspect, and I perceived it as my fault for making a tactical mistake. I should have cuffed him before I patted him down, but I put even more blame on myself by running those old voices through my head that were constantly repeating the things I had heard my entire life: *You can't do that because you are a girl. Women are weaker than men. Women should stay in their places.* I was unable to see myself as a warrior who had fought, been outnumbered, and come out alive. My inner strut had given me the strength to fight and not give up. That is what I am working on. That is what I hope to convey to my sisters. We win some; we lose some, but that doesn't make us the weaker sex. It makes us human.

At the time I was injured on the job, my son was seven. I began my career as a police officer when he was one and a half years old, and he had already been through his parents' divorce at six. I had started dating Billy a year after I was legally separated from his father, so my little boy had already been through a lot.

When I walked into my mom and dad's house to pick up my son after that shift with my shirt torn and nasty and my arm in a sling, my son's face reflected pure terror. He ran and grabbed me and held on for dear life. My dad's face went whiter than I have ever seen. When Billy got home from his fishing trip and saw my arm in a sling, he lost his ever-loving mind, and I had to remind him that things like that happened on the job.

Walking into my mom's kitchen that evening, battered and bruised, scared my little seven-year-old son so badly. It was the day I started telling myself I needed to leave police work if I wanted to raise my son. I was always aware of the chances we took every time we began a shift. However, my son's reaction marked the day I started seriously considering leaving police work. His clear worry for my safety was also coupled with the fact that all those people, whom I was supposed to be protecting from known drug dealers, had also just helped the bad guy escape (and this dealer had a record a half mile long). So I began questioning my purpose in this job. I mean, after all, why the hell should I try to protect people who would turn and help the ones I was trying to protect them from? Once again, I had survived another incident that could've ended badly for me, and my inner strut had channeled my warrior sisters and brought me out to the other side, relatively okay.

I was losing a lot of time with my son, and I didn't want to wake up one day knowing I'd lost his childhood years to my job. I also couldn't get the image of his face out of my head, that look he gave me when I walked in with my uniform dirty and my arm in a sling. He was terrified.

So what was I to do? This angry, warrior mom and wife who had lived her dream of becoming a police officer was now facing another challenge: fitting into normal society. The strut was going to have to be even stronger because this transition was not going to be easy, and little did I know that the battles I had fought were miniscule in comparison to the ones I had ahead of me.

AFTERWORD:

From Personal to Universal

From all of these personal stories I shared, I wish for women to know that we can overcome anything. We are strong. We are smart. We are capable. We need to claim our power and unleash our inner strut, live our dreams with no apologies. We need to understand that we have been lied to about our history. We have been led to believe that we are incapable of being exactly who we want to be, not knowing our true strut as a result. Instead, we need to see the power of our mothers and grandmothers and feel how that same power surges through us. We have the right to be and do whatever we choose, and once we realize that and connect with our sisters, the world will change because it will have no choice. We have all heard it said that we can change the world one person at a time, and I would like to add that if women opt to change the world one woman at a time, it will be a magnificent change indeed.

Every woman has a story that defines her spirit. Every woman can relate to a moment when she has been minimized, silenced, underestimated, and underrepresented. But at the same time, every woman has a story narrating obstacles, sometimes seemingly insurmountable, that she has overcome. We don't need to be men to claim this power, to claim our unique stories.

Our stories will provide the fertile ground for our daughters and sisters to know that we are unstoppable.

We are worthy.

We are enough.

We are warriors.

We are women.

PREVIEW FOR BOOK II

Respecting My Strut: Evolving on My Journey as a Woman Warrior

I was certainly a woman warrior as a cop. Little did I know that I would need to step up my warrior game when I hung up my shield for my son. My strut evolved into something I never dreamed possible. I dug deep in ways I had never imagined. I share these experiences in my next book.

As I began writing the first book, I realized what I was trying to accomplish would span more than one book, so the project evolved into a series. I wrestled with questions like: What is "being a woman"? What constitutes the behaviors and characteristics of women? These are the questions I found myself asking as I completed book I of this series.

We all say that we've come a long way toward equality for women and men, but I don't think so. When considering the history of women warriors who fought side by side with men on the battlefield that can be traced back to the fourth century, have we not actually regressed?

Along with the discovery of ourselves, if we allow it, can come true freedom, freedom without gender restrictions or lack of acceptance of others. We can all exist together if we mind our own business and allow others to do the same.

When I began my book, I didn't know what would come from my writing about women finding their strut. As with most writing, it began in one direction, but veered off into various other paths of discovery, including belief systems that I am still exploring. In the second book, I include stories from my life as I moved from being a cop to the civilian world into a new marriage blending two families, and one of the biggest losses of my life. The second book will take the reader through more of my self-discovery and evolution as I made my way through even more of life's challenges. I hope that by reading about my journey, other women can find their own way a little easier knowing that they aren't alone in their struggles, and that we are all warriors finding and demonstrating our strut.

Here is an excerpt from book II:

After ten years of a great marriage to my soul mate, we found out my husband, Billy, had cancer. He was diagnosed with lung cancer in the last week of May 2006, and he died the following January.

Those few months were some of the worst of my life. I won't describe all of the horrors of cancer, for many reasons. I will just say that these obstacles were harder than any I have ever encountered in my life before or since.

My son graduated from high school about a week before Billy was diagnosed. It was my son's dream to become a marine, so we knew what his plans were for after graduation. Right after Billy was diagnosed, even before we knew the prognosis, we sat my son down and told him that we didn't expect him to put his plans for joining up on hold. He should go ahead with his plans, so he did.

The marines, at least at that time, had a weird way of taking recruits to boot camp; they may still do it this way. They had a recruiter pick up these young people, who had signed away their independence to Uncle Sam, in the middle of the night. As I understand it, the purpose of this is to disorient them as they prepare them for the indoctrination of the military mindset.

I will never forget the feeling I had watching my baby boy walk out of the house at 3:00 a.m. to go to boot camp in Parris Island, South Carolina. while my husband lay dying on the couch. Just writing this felt difficult because of the pain of that night. I was looking at another transition period of my life, one that would be the hardest mountain I had ever scaled.

Follow me on Instagram @_karen_taylor to stay up to date and be among the first people notified when book II is released!

ABOUT THE AUTHOR

 Karen Taylor is a proud mother of a fine young man who served in the Marine Corps, and she is a dog lover to the point of ridiculousness. She loves reading books, spending time with her dogs, and basically being inappropriate. She is an English instructor at a community college in North Carolina and well known for being blunt, yet fiercely loyal to family, friends, students, and anyone who is a victim of a bully. You can connect with her on Instagram @_karen_taylor.